G000108938

ARE YOU ENJOYING THIS AWESOME BOOK?

If so, please leave us a review. We are very interested in your feedback to create even better products for you to enjoy in the near future.

Shopping for Aquarium Maintenance Logbook supplies can be fun. Discover our complete collection on our website at www.amazing-notebooks.com, our Amazon Page at http://bit.ly/amazing-notebooks or simply scan the QR code below to see all of our awesome and creative products!

THANK YOU VERY MUCH!

AMAZING NOTEBOOKS

www.amazing-notebooks.com

WELCOME TO YOUR WONDERFUL AQUARIUM MAINTENANCE LOGBOOK

NAME ....

PHONE ....

EMAIL ....

This notebook will help you to monitor and record all the details of your wonderful aquarium. You can easily add water testing like PH level, Ammonia, Nitrite, Nitrate and many more, filter water change and many more.

Monitoring your aquarium you can be sure it's in absolute optimum condition and you will avoid fish loss due to rising ammonia and nitrate levels.

Recommended Levels for Saltwater Aquariums

Parameters	Recommended Levels for Saltwater Aquariums	Average Levels for Coral Reefs
Temperature	24 – 27°C 75 – 80°F	27°C 82°F
Salinity	1.024 – 1.026 34 – 36 ppt	1.025 – 1.027 34 – 36 ppt
pH	7.8 – 8.4	8.0 – 8.3
Alkalinity	8 – 11dKH 150 – 200ppm	8dKH 150ppm
Calcium (Ca)	400 – 450ppm	420ppm
Ammonia (NH_3)	0ppm	< 0.1ppm
Nitrate (NO_3)	< 5ppm	< 0.1ppm
Phosphate (PO_4^{-3})	< 0.03ppm	0.005ppm
Magnesium (Mg)	1250 – 1400ppm	1300ppm
Iron (Fe)	Below Detection	0ppm
Iodine (I)	0.06-0.1ppm	0.06ppm
Strontium (Sr)	7-9ppm	8ppm
Boron (B)	< 10ppm	4.4ppm

Tank:	Days/Weeks Since the Last Test:
Date:	Fish count:	Fish Lost since the Last Count:
Fish Behavior:	Feeding:

Tick Box	Maintenance Check List	Maintenance check details
☐	**Filters Check**	
☐	**Pumps Check**	
☐	**Water Level**	
☐	**Water Temperature**	
☐	**Tubing Check**	
☐	**PH Level**	
☐	**Ammonia**	
☐	**Nitrite Level**	
☐	**Nitrate Level**	
☐	**Phosphate Level**	
☐	**Carbonate Hardness**	
☐	**Salinity Level**	
☐	**Calcium Level**	
☐	**Water Change** 10-15%	
☐	**Vaccum the Gravel**	
☐	**Check Lighting**	
☐	**Expiration dates** For Kits & Supplies	

ADDITIONAL NOTES

	Tank:		Days/Weeks Since the Last Test:

	Date:		Fish count:

	Fish Lost since the Last Count:

	Fish Behavior:		Feeding:

Tick Box	Maintenance Check List	Maintenance check details
☐	**Filters Check**	
☐	**Pumps Check**	
☐	**Water Level**	
☐	**Water Temperature**	
☐	**Tubing Check**	
☐	**PH Level**	
☐	**Ammonia**	
☐	**Nitrite Level**	
☐	**Nitrate Level**	
☐	**Phosphate Level**	
☐	**Carbonate Hardness**	
☐	**Salinity Level**	
☐	**Calcium Level**	
☐	**Water Change** 10-15%	
☐	**Vaccum the Gravel**	
☐	**Check Lighting**	
☐	**Expiration dates** For Kits & Supplies	

ADDITIONAL NOTES

	Tank:		Days/Weeks Since the Last Test:
	Date:	Fish count:	Fish Lost since the Last Count:
	Fish Behavior:		Feeding:

Tick Box	Maintenance Check List	Maintenance check details
☐	**Filters Check**	
☐	**Pumps Check**	
☐	**Water Level**	
☐	**Water Temperature**	
☐	**Tubing Check**	
☐	**PH Level**	
☐	**Ammonia**	
☐	**Nitrite Level**	
☐	**Nitrate Level**	
☐	**Phosphate Level**	
☐	**Carbonate Hardness**	
☐	**Salinity Level**	
☐	**Calcium Level**	
☐	**Water Change** 10-15%	
☐	**Vaccum the Gravel**	
☐	**Check Lighting**	
☐	**Expiration dates** For Kits & Supplies	

ADDITIONAL NOTES

| Tank: | Days/Weeks Since the Last Test: |

| Date: | Fish count: | Fish Lost since the Last Count: |

| Fish Behavior: | Feeding: |

Tick Box	Maintenance Check List	Maintenance check details
☐	Filters Check	
☐	Pumps Check	
☐	Water Level	
☐	Water Temperature	
☐	Tubing Check	
☐	PH Level	
☐	Ammonia	
☐	Nitrite Level	
☐	Nitrate Level	
☐	Phosphate Level	
☐	Carbonate Hardness	
☐	Salinity Level	
☐	Calcium Level	
☐	Water Change 10-15%	
☐	Vaccum the Gravel	
☐	Check Lighting	
☐	Expiration dates For Kits & Supplies	

ADDITIONAL NOTES

	Tank:		Days/Weeks Since the Last Test:
	Date:	Fish count:	Fish Lost since the Last Count:
	Fish Behavior:		Feeding:

Tick Box	Maintenance Check List	Maintenance check details
☐	**Filters Check**	
☐	**Pumps Check**	
☐	**Water Level**	
☐	**Water Temperature**	
☐	**Tubing Check**	
☐	**PH Level**	
☐	**Ammonia**	
☐	**Nitrite Level**	
☐	**Nitrate Level**	
☐	**Phosphate Level**	
☐	**Carbonate Hardness**	
☐	**Salinity Level**	
☐	**Calcium Level**	
☐	**Water Change** 10-15%	
☐	**Vaccum the Gravel**	
☐	**Check Lighting**	
☐	**Expiration dates** For Kits & Supplies	

ADDITIONAL NOTES

Tank:		Days/Weeks Since the Last Test:
Date:	Fish count:	Fish Lost since the Last Count:
Fish Behavior:		Feeding:

Tick Box	Maintenance Check List	Maintenance check details
☐	**Filters Check**	
☐	**Pumps Check**	
☐	**Water Level**	
☐	**Water Temperature**	
☐	**Tubing Check**	
☐	**PH Level**	
☐	**Ammonia**	
☐	**Nitrite Level**	
☐	**Nitrate Level**	
☐	**Phosphate Level**	
☐	**Carbonate Hardness**	
☐	**Salinity Level**	
☐	**Calcium Level**	
☐	**Water Change** 10-15%	
☐	**Vaccum the Gravel**	
☐	**Check Lighting**	
☐	**Expiration dates** For Kits & Supplies	

ADDITIONAL NOTES

	Tank:			Days/Weeks Since the Last Test:

	Date:		Fish count:		Fish Lost since the Last Count:

	Fish Behavior:			Feeding:

Tick Box	Maintenance Check List	Maintenance check details
☐	**Filters Check**	....
☐	**Pumps Check**	....
☐	**Water Level**	....
☐	**Water Temperature**	....
☐	**Tubing Check**	....
☐	**PH Level**	....
☐	**Ammonia**	....
☐	**Nitrite Level**	....
☐	**Nitrate Level**	....
☐	**Phosphate Level**	....
☐	**Carbonate Hardness**	....
☐	**Salinity Level**	....
☐	**Calcium Level**	....
☐	**Water Change** 10-15%	....
☐	**Vaccum the Gravel**	....
☐	**Check Lighting**	....
☐	**Expiration dates** For Kits & Supplies	....

ADDITIONAL NOTES

Tank:		Days/Weeks Since the Last Test:
Date:	Fish count:	Fish Lost since the Last Count:
Fish Behavior:		Feeding:

Tick Box	Maintenance Check List	Maintenance check details
☐	**Filters Check**	
☐	**Pumps Check**	
☐	**Water Level**	
☐	**Water Temperature**	
☐	**Tubing Check**	
☐	**PH Level**	
☐	**Ammonia**	
☐	**Nitrite Level**	
☐	**Nitrate Level**	
☐	**Phosphate Level**	
☐	**Carbonate Hardness**	
☐	**Salinity Level**	
☐	**Calcium Level**	
☐	**Water Change** 10-15%	
☐	**Vaccum the Gravel**	
☐	**Check Lighting**	
☐	**Expiration dates** For Kits & Supplies	

ADDITIONAL NOTES

	Tank:			Days/Weeks Since the Last Test:
	Date:		Fish count:	Fish Lost since the Last Count:
	Fish Behavior:			Feeding:

Tick Box	Maintenance Check List	Maintenance check details
☐	**Filters Check**	
☐	**Pumps Check**	
☐	**Water Level**	
☐	**Water Temperature**	
☐	**Tubing Check**	
☐	**PH Level**	
☐	**Ammonia**	
☐	**Nitrite Level**	
☐	**Nitrate Level**	
☐	**Phosphate Level**	
☐	**Carbonate Hardness**	
☐	**Salinity Level**	
☐	**Calcium Level**	
☐	**Water Change** 10-15%	
☐	**Vaccum the Gravel**	
☐	**Check Lighting**	
☐	**Expiration dates** For Kits & Supplies	

ADDITIONAL NOTES

Tank:		Days/Weeks Since the Last Test:
Date:	Fish count:	Fish Lost since the Last Count:
Fish Behavior:		Feeding:

Tick Box	Maintenance Check List	Maintenance check details
☐	**Filters Check**	
☐	**Pumps Check**	
☐	**Water Level**	
☐	**Water Temperature**	
☐	**Tubing Check**	
☐	**PH Level**	
☐	**Ammonia**	
☐	**Nitrite Level**	
☐	**Nitrate Level**	
☐	**Phosphate Level**	
☐	**Carbonate Hardness**	
☐	**Salinity Level**	
☐	**Calcium Level**	
☐	**Water Change** 10-15%	
☐	**Vaccum the Gravel**	
☐	**Check Lighting**	
☐	**Expiration dates** For Kits & Supplies	

ADDITIONAL NOTES

| Tank: | Days/Weeks Since the Last Test: |

| Date: | Fish count: | Fish Lost since the Last Count: |

| Fish Behavior: | Feeding: |

Tick Box	Maintenance Check List	Maintenance check details
☐	**Filters Check**	
☐	**Pumps Check**	
☐	**Water Level**	
☐	**Water Temperature**	
☐	**Tubing Check**	
☐	**PH Level**	
☐	**Ammonia**	
☐	**Nitrite Level**	
☐	**Nitrate Level**	
☐	**Phosphate Level**	
☐	**Carbonate Hardness**	
☐	**Salinity Level**	
☐	**Calcium Level**	
☐	**Water Change** 10-15%	
☐	**Vaccum the Gravel**	
☐	**Check Lighting**	
☐	**Expiration dates** For Kits & Supplies	

ADDITIONAL NOTES

Tank:		Days/Weeks Since the Last Test:
Date:	Fish count:	Fish Lost since the Last Count:
Fish Behavior:		Feeding:

Tick Box	Maintenance Check List	Maintenance check details
☐	**Filters Check**	
☐	**Pumps Check**	
☐	**Water Level**	
☐	**Water Temperature**	
☐	**Tubing Check**	
☐	**PH Level**	
☐	**Ammonia**	
☐	**Nitrite Level**	
☐	**Nitrate Level**	
☐	**Phosphate Level**	
☐	**Carbonate Hardness**	
☐	**Salinity Level**	
☐	**Calcium Level**	
☐	**Water Change** 10-15%	
☐	**Vaccum the Gravel**	
☐	**Check Lighting**	
☐	**Expiration dates** For Kits & Supplies	

ADDITIONAL NOTES

Tank:		Days/Weeks Since the Last Test:
Date:	Fish count:	Fish Lost since the Last Count:
Fish Behavior:		Feeding:

Tick Box	Maintenance Check List	Maintenance check details
☐	**Filters Check**	
☐	**Pumps Check**	
☐	**Water Level**	
☐	**Water Temperature**	
☐	**Tubing Check**	
☐	**PH Level**	
☐	**Ammonia**	
☐	**Nitrite Level**	
☐	**Nitrate Level**	
☐	**Phosphate Level**	
☐	**Carbonate Hardness**	
☐	**Salinity Level**	
☐	**Calcium Level**	
☐	**Water Change** 10-15%	
☐	**Vaccum the Gravel**	
☐	**Check Lighting**	
☐	**Expiration dates** For Kits & Supplies	

ADDITIONAL NOTES

	Tank:		Days/Weeks Since the Last Test:
	Date:	Fish count:	Fish Lost since the Last Count:
	Fish Behavior:		Feeding:

Tick Box	Maintenance Check List	Maintenance check details
☐	**Filters Check**	
☐	**Pumps Check**	
☐	**Water Level**	
☐	**Water Temperature**	
☐	**Tubing Check**	
☐	**PH Level**	
☐	**Ammonia**	
☐	**Nitrite Level**	
☐	**Nitrate Level**	
☐	**Phosphate Level**	
☐	**Carbonate Hardness**	
☐	**Salinity Level**	
☐	**Calcium Level**	
☐	**Water Change** 10-15%	
☐	**Vaccum the Gravel**	
☐	**Check Lighting**	
☐	**Expiration dates** For Kits & Supplies	

ADDITIONAL NOTES

	Tank:		Days/Weeks Since the Last Test:
	Date:	Fish count:	Fish Lost since the Last Count:
	Fish Behavior:		Feeding:

Tick Box	Maintenance Check List	Maintenance check details
☐	**Filters Check**	
☐	**Pumps Check**	
☐	**Water Level**	
☐	**Water Temperature**	
☐	**Tubing Check**	
☐	**PH Level**	
☐	**Ammonia**	
☐	**Nitrite Level**	
☐	**Nitrate Level**	
☐	**Phosphate Level**	
☐	**Carbonate Hardness**	
☐	**Salinity Level**	
☐	**Calcium Level**	
☐	**Water Change** 10-15%	
☐	**Vaccum the Gravel**	
☐	**Check Lighting**	
☐	**Expiration dates** For Kits & Supplies	

ADDITIONAL NOTES

	Tank:		Days/Weeks Since the Last Test:

	Date:		Fish count:		Fish Lost since the Last Count:

	Fish Behavior:		Feeding:

Tick Box	Maintenance Check List	Maintenance check details
☐	**Filters Check**	
☐	**Pumps Check**	
☐	**Water Level**	
☐	**Water Temperature**	
☐	**Tubing Check**	
☐	**PH Level**	
☐	**Ammonia**	
☐	**Nitrite Level**	
☐	**Nitrate Level**	
☐	**Phosphate Level**	
☐	**Carbonate Hardness**	
☐	**Salinity Level**	
☐	**Calcium Level**	
☐	**Water Change** 10-15%	
☐	**Vaccum the Gravel**	
☐	**Check Lighting**	
☐	**Expiration dates** For Kits & Supplies	

ADDITIONAL NOTES

	Tank:				Days/Weeks Since the Last Test:

	Date:			Fish count:			Fish Lost since the Last Count:

	Fish Behavior:			Feeding:

Tick Box	Maintenance Check List	Maintenance check details
☐	**Filters Check**	
☐	**Pumps Check**	
☐	**Water Level**	
☐	**Water Temperature**	
☐	**Tubing Check**	
☐	**PH Level**	
☐	**Ammonia**	
☐	**Nitrite Level**	
☐	**Nitrate Level**	
☐	**Phosphate Level**	
☐	**Carbonate Hardness**	
☐	**Salinity Level**	
☐	**Calcium Level**	
☐	**Water Change** 10-15%	
☐	**Vaccum the Gravel**	
☐	**Check Lighting**	
☐	**Expiration dates** For Kits & Supplies	

ADDITIONAL NOTES

Tank:		Days/Weeks Since the Last Test:
Date:	Fish count:	Fish Lost since the Last Count:
Fish Behavior:		Feeding:

Tick Box	Maintenance Check List	Maintenance check details
☐	**Filters Check**	
☐	**Pumps Check**	
☐	**Water Level**	
☐	**Water Temperature**	
☐	**Tubing Check**	
☐	**PH Level**	
☐	**Ammonia**	
☐	**Nitrite Level**	
☐	**Nitrate Level**	
☐	**Phosphate Level**	
☐	**Carbonate Hardness**	
☐	**Salinity Level**	
☐	**Calcium Level**	
☐	**Water Change** 10-15%	
☐	**Vaccum the Gravel**	
☐	**Check Lighting**	
☐	**Expiration dates** For Kits & Supplies	

ADDITIONAL NOTES

	Tank:		Days/Weeks Since the Last Test:
	Date:	Fish count:	Fish Lost since the Last Count:
	Fish Behavior:		Feeding:

Tick Box	Maintenance Check List	Maintenance check details
☐	**Filters Check**	
☐	**Pumps Check**	
☐	**Water Level**	
☐	**Water Temperature**	
☐	**Tubing Check**	
☐	**PH Level**	
☐	**Ammonia**	
☐	**Nitrite Level**	
☐	**Nitrate Level**	
☐	**Phosphate Level**	
☐	**Carbonate Hardness**	
☐	**Salinity Level**	
☐	**Calcium Level**	
☐	**Water Change** 10-15%	
☐	**Vaccum the Gravel**	
☐	**Check Lighting**	
☐	**Expiration dates** For Kits & Supplies	

ADDITIONAL NOTES

	Tank:		Days/Weeks Since the Last Test:

	Date:		Fish count:		Fish Lost since the Last Count:

	Fish Behavior:		Feeding:

Tick Box	Maintenance Check List	Maintenance check details
☐	**Filters Check**	
☐	**Pumps Check**	
☐	**Water Level**	
☐	**Water Temperature**	
☐	**Tubing Check**	
☐	**PH Level**	
☐	**Ammonia**	
☐	**Nitrite Level**	
☐	**Nitrate Level**	
☐	**Phosphate Level**	
☐	**Carbonate Hardness**	
☐	**Salinity Level**	
☐	**Calcium Level**	
☐	**Water Change** 10-15%	
☐	**Vaccum the Gravel**	
☐	**Check Lighting**	
☐	**Expiration dates** For Kits & Supplies	

ADDITIONAL NOTES

Tank:		Days/Weeks Since the Last Test:
Date:	Fish count:	Fish Lost since the Last Count:
Fish Behavior:		Feeding:

Tick Box	Maintenance Check List	Maintenance check details
☐	**Filters Check**	
☐	**Pumps Check**	
☐	**Water Level**	
☐	**Water Temperature**	
☐	**Tubing Check**	
☐	**PH Level**	
☐	**Ammonia**	
☐	**Nitrite Level**	
☐	**Nitrate Level**	
☐	**Phosphate Level**	
☐	**Carbonate Hardness**	
☐	**Salinity Level**	
☐	**Calcium Level**	
☐	**Water Change** 10-15%	
☐	**Vaccum the Gravel**	
☐	**Check Lighting**	
☐	**Expiration dates** For Kits & Supplies	

ADDITIONAL NOTES

Tank:		Days/Weeks Since the Last Test:
Date:	Fish count:	Fish Lost since the Last Count:
Fish Behavior:		Feeding:

Tick Box	Maintenance Check List	Maintenance check details
☐	**Filters Check**	
☐	**Pumps Check**	
☐	**Water Level**	
☐	**Water Temperature**	
☐	**Tubing Check**	
☐	**PH Level**	
☐	**Ammonia**	
☐	**Nitrite Level**	
☐	**Nitrate Level**	
☐	**Phosphate Level**	
☐	**Carbonate Hardness**	
☐	**Salinity Level**	
☐	**Calcium Level**	
☐	**Water Change** 10-15%	
☐	**Vaccum the Gravel**	
☐	**Check Lighting**	
☐	**Expiration dates** For Kits & Supplies	

ADDITIONAL NOTES

Tank:		Days/Weeks Since the Last Test:
Date:	Fish count:	Fish Lost since the Last Count:
Fish Behavior:		Feeding:

Tick Box	Maintenance Check List	Maintenance check details
☐	**Filters Check**	
☐	**Pumps Check**	
☐	**Water Level**	
☐	**Water Temperature**	
☐	**Tubing Check**	
☐	**PH Level**	
☐	**Ammonia**	
☐	**Nitrite Level**	
☐	**Nitrate Level**	
☐	**Phosphate Level**	
☐	**Carbonate Hardness**	
☐	**Salinity Level**	
☐	**Calcium Level**	
☐	**Water Change** 10-15%	
☐	**Vaccum the Gravel**	
☐	**Check Lighting**	
☐	**Expiration dates** For Kits & Supplies	

ADDITIONAL NOTES

	Tank:		Days/Weeks Since the Last Test:

	Date:		Fish count:

Fish Lost since the Last Count:

Fish Behavior:

Feeding:

Tick Box	Maintenance Check List	Maintenance check details
☐	**Filters Check**	
☐	**Pumps Check**	
☐	**Water Level**	
☐	**Water Temperature**	
☐	**Tubing Check**	
☐	**PH Level**	
☐	**Ammonia**	
☐	**Nitrite Level**	
☐	**Nitrate Level**	
☐	**Phosphate Level**	
☐	**Carbonate Hardness**	
☐	**Salinity Level**	
☐	**Calcium Level**	
☐	**Water Change** 10-15%	
☐	**Vaccum the Gravel**	
☐	**Check Lighting**	
☐	**Expiration dates** For Kits & Supplies	

ADDITIONAL NOTES

Tank:		Days/Weeks Since the Last Test:

Date:	Fish count:	Fish Lost since the Last Count:

Fish Behavior:	Feeding:

Tick Box	Maintenance Check List	Maintenance check details
☐	**Filters Check**	
☐	**Pumps Check**	
☐	**Water Level**	
☐	**Water Temperature**	
☐	**Tubing Check**	
☐	**PH Level**	
☐	**Ammonia**	
☐	**Nitrite Level**	
☐	**Nitrate Level**	
☐	**Phosphate Level**	
☐	**Carbonate Hardness**	
☐	**Salinity Level**	
☐	**Calcium Level**	
☐	**Water Change** 10-15%	
☐	**Vaccum the Gravel**	
☐	**Check Lighting**	
☐	**Expiration dates** For Kits & Supplies	

ADDITIONAL NOTES

	Tank:		Days/Weeks Since the Last Test:

	Date:		Fish count:

	Fish Lost since the Last Count:

	Fish Behavior:		Feeding:

Tick Box	Maintenance Check List	Maintenance check details
☐	**Filters Check**	
☐	**Pumps Check**	
☐	**Water Level**	
☐	**Water Temperature**	
☐	**Tubing Check**	
☐	**PH Level**	
☐	**Ammonia**	
☐	**Nitrite Level**	
☐	**Nitrate Level**	
☐	**Phosphate Level**	
☐	**Carbonate Hardness**	
☐	**Salinity Level**	
☐	**Calcium Level**	
☐	**Water Change** 10-15%	
☐	**Vaccum the Gravel**	
☐	**Check Lighting**	
☐	**Expiration dates** For Kits & Supplies	

ADDITIONAL NOTES

	Tank:			Days/Weeks Since the Last Test:

	Date:		Fish count:		Fish Lost since the Last Count:

	Fish Behavior:			Feeding:

Tick Box	Maintenance Check List	Maintenance check details
☐	**Filters Check**	
☐	**Pumps Check**	
☐	**Water Level**	
☐	**Water Temperature**	
☐	**Tubing Check**	
☐	**PH Level**	
☐	**Ammonia**	
☐	**Nitrite Level**	
☐	**Nitrate Level**	
☐	**Phosphate Level**	
☐	**Carbonate Hardness**	
☐	**Salinity Level**	
☐	**Calcium Level**	
☐	**Water Change** 10-15%	
☐	**Vaccum the Gravel**	
☐	**Check Lighting**	
☐	**Expiration dates** For Kits & Supplies	

ADDITIONAL NOTES

	Tank:			Days/Weeks Since the Last Test:

Tank:

Days/Weeks Since the Last Test:

Date: Fish count:

Fish Lost since the Last Count:

Fish Behavior:

Feeding:

Tick Box	Maintenance Check List	Maintenance check details
☐	**Filters Check**	
☐	**Pumps Check**	
☐	**Water Level**	
☐	**Water Temperature**	
☐	**Tubing Check**	
☐	**PH Level**	
☐	**Ammonia**	
☐	**Nitrite Level**	
☐	**Nitrate Level**	
☐	**Phosphate Level**	
☐	**Carbonate Hardness**	
☐	**Salinity Level**	
☐	**Calcium Level**	
☐	**Water Change** 10-15%	
☐	**Vaccum the Gravel**	
☐	**Check Lighting**	
☐	**Expiration dates** For Kits & Supplies	

ADDITIONAL NOTES

Tank:		Days/Weeks Since the Last Test:
Date:	Fish count:	Fish Lost since the Last Count:
Fish Behavior:		Feeding:

Tick Box	Maintenance Check List	Maintenance check details
☐	**Filters Check**	
☐	**Pumps Check**	
☐	**Water Level**	
☐	**Water Temperature**	
☐	**Tubing Check**	
☐	**PH Level**	
☐	**Ammonia**	
☐	**Nitrite Level**	
☐	**Nitrate Level**	
☐	**Phosphate Level**	
☐	**Carbonate Hardness**	
☐	**Salinity Level**	
☐	**Calcium Level**	
☐	**Water Change** 10-15%	
☐	**Vaccum the Gravel**	
☐	**Check Lighting**	
☐	**Expiration dates** For Kits & Supplies	

ADDITIONAL NOTES

Tank:		Days/Weeks Since the Last Test:
Date:	Fish count:	Fish Lost since the Last Count:
Fish Behavior:		Feeding:

Tick Box	Maintenance Check List	Maintenance check details
☐	**Filters Check**	
☐	**Pumps Check**	
☐	**Water Level**	
☐	**Water Temperature**	
☐	**Tubing Check**	
☐	**PH Level**	
☐	**Ammonia**	
☐	**Nitrite Level**	
☐	**Nitrate Level**	
☐	**Phosphate Level**	
☐	**Carbonate Hardness**	
☐	**Salinity Level**	
☐	**Calcium Level**	
☐	**Water Change** 10-15%	
☐	**Vaccum the Gravel**	
☐	**Check Lighting**	
☐	**Expiration dates** For Kits & Supplies	

ADDITIONAL NOTES

	Tank:		Days/Weeks Since the Last Test:
	Date:	Fish count:	Fish Lost since the Last Count:
	Fish Behavior:		Feeding:

Tick Box	Maintenance Check List	Maintenance check details
☐	**Filters Check**	
☐	**Pumps Check**	
☐	**Water Level**	
☐	**Water Temperature**	
☐	**Tubing Check**	
☐	**PH Level**	
☐	**Ammonia**	
☐	**Nitrite Level**	
☐	**Nitrate Level**	
☐	**Phosphate Level**	
☐	**Carbonate Hardness**	
☐	**Salinity Level**	
☐	**Calcium Level**	
☐	**Water Change** 10-15%	
☐	**Vaccum the Gravel**	
☐	**Check Lighting**	
☐	**Expiration dates** For Kits & Supplies	

ADDITIONAL NOTES

	Tank:		Days/Weeks Since the Last Test:
Date:	Fish count:	Fish Lost since the Last Count:
Fish Behavior:		Feeding:

Tick Box	Maintenance Check List	Maintenance check details
☐	**Filters Check**	
☐	**Pumps Check**	
☐	**Water Level**	
☐	**Water Temperature**	
☐	**Tubing Check**	
☐	**PH Level**	
☐	**Ammonia**	
☐	**Nitrite Level**	
☐	**Nitrate Level**	
☐	**Phosphate Level**	
☐	**Carbonate Hardness**	
☐	**Salinity Level**	
☐	**Calcium Level**	
☐	**Water Change** 10-15%	
☐	**Vaccum the Gravel**	
☐	**Check Lighting**	
☐	**Expiration dates** For Kits & Supplies	

ADDITIONAL NOTES

🐠 Tank:		📅 Days/Weeks Since the Last Test:
📅 Date:	🐟 Fish count:	Fish Lost since the Last Count:
🌵 Fish Behavior:		🐟 Feeding:

Tick Box	Maintenance Check List	Maintenance check details
☐	**Filters Check**	....
☐	**Pumps Check**	....
☐	**Water Level**	....
☐	**Water Temperature**	....
☐	**Tubing Check**	....
☐	**PH Level**	....
☐	**Ammonia**	....
☐	**Nitrite Level**	....
☐	**Nitrate Level**	....
☐	**Phosphate Level**	....
☐	**Carbonate Hardness**	....
☐	**Salinity Level**	....
☐	**Calcium Level**	....
☐	**Water Change** 10-15%	....
☐	**Vaccum the Gravel**	....
☐	**Check Lighting**	....
☐	**Expiration dates** For Kits & Supplies	....

ADDITIONAL NOTES

Tank:	Days/Weeks Since the Last Test:
Date:	Fish count:
Fish Behavior:	Fish Lost since the Last Count:
	Feeding:

Tick Box	Maintenance Check List	Maintenance check details
☐	**Filters Check**	
☐	**Pumps Check**	
☐	**Water Level**	
☐	**Water Temperature**	
☐	**Tubing Check**	
☐	**PH Level**	
☐	**Ammonia**	
☐	**Nitrite Level**	
☐	**Nitrate Level**	
☐	**Phosphate Level**	
☐	**Carbonate Hardness**	
☐	**Salinity Level**	
☐	**Calcium Level**	
☐	**Water Change** 10-15%	
☐	**Vaccum the Gravel**	
☐	**Check Lighting**	
☐	**Expiration dates** For Kits & Supplies	

ADDITIONAL NOTES

🐠 Tank:		📅 Days/Weeks Since the Last Test:
📅 Date:	🐟 Fish count:	🖥️ Fish Lost since the Last Count:
🐠 Fish Behavior:		🐠 Feeding:

Tick Box	Maintenance Check List	Maintenance check details
☐	**Filters Check**	....
☐	**Pumps Check**	....
☐	**Water Level**	....
☐	**Water Temperature**	....
☐	**Tubing Check**	....
☐	**PH Level**	....
☐	**Ammonia**	....
☐	**Nitrite Level**	....
☐	**Nitrate Level**	....
☐	**Phosphate Level**	....
☐	**Carbonate Hardness**	....
☐	**Salinity Level**	....
☐	**Calcium Level**	....
☐	**Water Change** 10-15%	....
☐	**Vaccum the Gravel**	....
☐	**Check Lighting**	....
☐	**Expiration dates** For Kits & Supplies	....

ADDITIONAL NOTES

Tank:		Days/Weeks Since the Last Test:

Date:	Fish count:

Fish Lost since the Last Count:

Fish Behavior:	Feeding:

Tick Box	Maintenance Check List	Maintenance check details
☐	**Filters Check**	
☐	**Pumps Check**	
☐	**Water Level**	
☐	**Water Temperature**	
☐	**Tubing Check**	
☐	**PH Level**	
☐	**Ammonia**	
☐	**Nitrite Level**	
☐	**Nitrate Level**	
☐	**Phosphate Level**	
☐	**Carbonate Hardness**	
☐	**Salinity Level**	
☐	**Calcium Level**	
☐	**Water Change** 10-15%	
☐	**Vaccum the Gravel**	
☐	**Check Lighting**	
☐	**Expiration dates** For Kits & Supplies	

ADDITIONAL NOTES

Tank:

Days/Weeks Since the Last Test:

Date:

Fish count:

Fish Lost since the Last Count:

Fish Behavior:

Feeding:

Tick Box	Maintenance Check List	Maintenance check details
☐	**Filters Check**	
☐	**Pumps Check**	
☐	**Water Level**	
☐	**Water Temperature**	
☐	**Tubing Check**	
☐	**PH Level**	
☐	**Ammonia**	
☐	**Nitrite Level**	
☐	**Nitrate Level**	
☐	**Phosphate Level**	
☐	**Carbonate Hardness**	
☐	**Salinity Level**	
☐	**Calcium Level**	
☐	**Water Change** 10-15%	
☐	**Vaccum the Gravel**	
☐	**Check Lighting**	
☐	**Expiration dates** For Kits & Supplies	

ADDITIONAL NOTES

	Tank:		Days/Weeks Since the Last Test:
	Date:	Fish count:	Fish Lost since the Last Count:
	Fish Behavior:		Feeding:

Tick Box	Maintenance Check List	Maintenance check details
☐	**Filters Check**	
☐	**Pumps Check**	
☐	**Water Level**	
☐	**Water Temperature**	
☐	**Tubing Check**	
☐	**PH Level**	
☐	**Ammonia**	
☐	**Nitrite Level**	
☐	**Nitrate Level**	
☐	**Phosphate Level**	
☐	**Carbonate Hardness**	
☐	**Salinity Level**	
☐	**Calcium Level**	
☐	**Water Change** 10-15%	
☐	**Vaccum the Gravel**	
☐	**Check Lighting**	
☐	**Expiration dates** For Kits & Supplies	

ADDITIONAL NOTES

Tank:		Days/Weeks Since the Last Test:
Date:	Fish count:	Fish Lost since the Last Count:
Fish Behavior:		Feeding:

Tick Box	Maintenance Check List	Maintenance check details
☐	**Filters Check**	
☐	**Pumps Check**	
☐	**Water Level**	
☐	**Water Temperature**	
☐	**Tubing Check**	
☐	**PH Level**	
☐	**Ammonia**	
☐	**Nitrite Level**	
☐	**Nitrate Level**	
☐	**Phosphate Level**	
☐	**Carbonate Hardness**	
☐	**Salinity Level**	
☐	**Calcium Level**	
☐	**Water Change** 10-15%	
☐	**Vaccum the Gravel**	
☐	**Check Lighting**	
☐	**Expiration dates** For Kits & Supplies	

ADDITIONAL NOTES

	Tank:		Days/Weeks Since the Last Test:
	Date:	Fish count:	Fish Lost since the Last Count:
	Fish Behavior:		Feeding:

Tick Box	Maintenance Check List	Maintenance check details
☐	**Filters Check**	
☐	**Pumps Check**	
☐	**Water Level**	
☐	**Water Temperature**	
☐	**Tubing Check**	
☐	**PH Level**	
☐	**Ammonia**	
☐	**Nitrite Level**	
☐	**Nitrate Level**	
☐	**Phosphate Level**	
☐	**Carbonate Hardness**	
☐	**Salinity Level**	
☐	**Calcium Level**	
☐	**Water Change** 10-15%	
☐	**Vaccum the Gravel**	
☐	**Check Lighting**	
☐	**Expiration dates** For Kits & Supplies	

ADDITIONAL NOTES

Tank:		Days/Weeks Since the Last Test:
Date:	Fish count:	Fish Lost since the Last Count:
Fish Behavior:		Feeding:

Tick Box	Maintenance Check List	Maintenance check details
☐	**Filters Check**	....
☐	**Pumps Check**	....
☐	**Water Level**	....
☐	**Water Temperature**	....
☐	**Tubing Check**	....
☐	**PH Level**	....
☐	**Ammonia**	....
☐	**Nitrite Level**	....
☐	**Nitrate Level**	....
☐	**Phosphate Level**	....
☐	**Carbonate Hardness**	....
☐	**Salinity Level**	....
☐	**Calcium Level**	....
☐	**Water Change** 10-15%	....
☐	**Vaccum the Gravel**	....
☐	**Check Lighting**	....
☐	**Expiration dates** For Kits & Supplies	....

ADDITIONAL NOTES

	Tank:		Days/Weeks Since the Last Test:
	Date:	Fish count:	Fish Lost since the Last Count:
	Fish Behavior:		Feeding:

Tick Box	Maintenance Check List	Maintenance check details
☐	**Filters Check**	
☐	**Pumps Check**	
☐	**Water Level**	
☐	**Water Temperature**	
☐	**Tubing Check**	
☐	**PH Level**	
☐	**Ammonia**	
☐	**Nitrite Level**	
☐	**Nitrate Level**	
☐	**Phosphate Level**	
☐	**Carbonate Hardness**	
☐	**Salinity Level**	
☐	**Calcium Level**	
☐	**Water Change** 10-15%	
☐	**Vaccum the Gravel**	
☐	**Check Lighting**	
☐	**Expiration dates** For Kits & Supplies	

ADDITIONAL NOTES

	Tank:		Days/Weeks Since the Last Test:
	Date:	Fish count:	Fish Lost since the Last Count:
	Fish Behavior:		Feeding:

Tick Box	Maintenance Check List	Maintenance check details
☐	**Filters Check**	....
☐	**Pumps Check**	....
☐	**Water Level**	....
☐	**Water Temperature**	....
☐	**Tubing Check**	....
☐	**PH Level**	....
☐	**Ammonia**	....
☐	**Nitrite Level**	....
☐	**Nitrate Level**	....
☐	**Phosphate Level**	....
☐	**Carbonate Hardness**	....
☐	**Salinity Level**	....
☐	**Calcium Level**	....
☐	**Water Change** 10-15%	....
☐	**Vaccum the Gravel**	....
☐	**Check Lighting**	....
☐	**Expiration dates** For Kits & Supplies	....

ADDITIONAL NOTES

Tank:		Days/Weeks Since the Last Test:
Date:	Fish count:	Fish Lost since the Last Count:
Fish Behavior:		Feeding:

Tick Box	Maintenance Check List	Maintenance check details
☐	**Filters Check**	
☐	**Pumps Check**	
☐	**Water Level**	
☐	**Water Temperature**	
☐	**Tubing Check**	
☐	**PH Level**	
☐	**Ammonia**	
☐	**Nitrite Level**	
☐	**Nitrate Level**	
☐	**Phosphate Level**	
☐	**Carbonate Hardness**	
☐	**Salinity Level**	
☐	**Calcium Level**	
☐	**Water Change** 10-15%	
☐	**Vaccum the Gravel**	
☐	**Check Lighting**	
☐	**Expiration dates** For Kits & Supplies	

ADDITIONAL NOTES

Tank:		Days/Weeks Since the Last Test:

Date: | Fish count: | Fish Lost since the Last Count:

Fish Behavior: | Feeding:

Tick Box	Maintenance Check List	Maintenance check details
☐	**Filters Check**	
☐	**Pumps Check**	
☐	**Water Level**	
☐	**Water Temperature**	
☐	**Tubing Check**	
☐	**PH Level**	
☐	**Ammonia**	
☐	**Nitrite Level**	
☐	**Nitrate Level**	
☐	**Phosphate Level**	
☐	**Carbonate Hardness**	
☐	**Salinity Level**	
☐	**Calcium Level**	
☐	**Water Change** 10-15%	
☐	**Vaccum the Gravel**	
☐	**Check Lighting**	
☐	**Expiration dates** For Kits & Supplies	

ADDITIONAL NOTES

	Tank:		Days/Weeks Since the Last Test:

	Date:		Fish count:		Fish Lost since the Last Count:

	Fish Behavior:		Feeding:

Tick Box	Maintenance Check List	Maintenance check details
☐	**Filters Check**	
☐	**Pumps Check**	
☐	**Water Level**	
☐	**Water Temperature**	
☐	**Tubing Check**	
☐	**PH Level**	
☐	**Ammonia**	
☐	**Nitrite Level**	
☐	**Nitrate Level**	
☐	**Phosphate Level**	
☐	**Carbonate Hardness**	
☐	**Salinity Level**	
☐	**Calcium Level**	
☐	**Water Change** 10-15%	
☐	**Vaccum the Gravel**	
☐	**Check Lighting**	
☐	**Expiration dates** For Kits & Supplies	

ADDITIONAL NOTES

Tank:	Days/Weeks Since the Last Test:
Date:	Fish count:	Fish Lost since the Last Count:
Fish Behavior:	Feeding:

Tick Box	Maintenance Check List	Maintenance check details
☐	**Filters Check**	
☐	**Pumps Check**	
☐	**Water Level**	
☐	**Water Temperature**	
☐	**Tubing Check**	
☐	**PH Level**	
☐	**Ammonia**	
☐	**Nitrite Level**	
☐	**Nitrate Level**	
☐	**Phosphate Level**	
☐	**Carbonate Hardness**	
☐	**Salinity Level**	
☐	**Calcium Level**	
☐	**Water Change** 10-15%	
☐	**Vaccum the Gravel**	
☐	**Check Lighting**	
☐	**Expiration dates** For Kits & Supplies	

ADDITIONAL NOTES

	Tank:		Days/Weeks Since the Last Test:
	Date:	Fish count:	Fish Lost since the Last Count:
	Fish Behavior:		Feeding:

Tick Box	Maintenance Check List	Maintenance check details
☐	**Filters Check**	
☐	**Pumps Check**	
☐	**Water Level**	
☐	**Water Temperature**	
☐	**Tubing Check**	
☐	**PH Level**	
☐	**Ammonia**	
☐	**Nitrite Level**	
☐	**Nitrate Level**	
☐	**Phosphate Level**	
☐	**Carbonate Hardness**	
☐	**Salinity Level**	
☐	**Calcium Level**	
☐	**Water Change** 10-15%	
☐	**Vaccum the Gravel**	
☐	**Check Lighting**	
☐	**Expiration dates** For Kits & Supplies	

ADDITIONAL NOTES

	Tank:			Days/Weeks Since the Last Test:

	Date:		Fish count:		Fish Lost since the Last Count:

	Fish Behavior:			Feeding:

Tick Box	Maintenance Check List	Maintenance check details
☐	**Filters Check**	....
☐	**Pumps Check**	....
☐	**Water Level**	....
☐	**Water Temperature**	....
☐	**Tubing Check**	....
☐	**PH Level**	....
☐	**Ammonia**	....
☐	**Nitrite Level**	....
☐	**Nitrate Level**	....
☐	**Phosphate Level**	....
☐	**Carbonate Hardness**	....
☐	**Salinity Level**	....
☐	**Calcium Level**	....
☐	**Water Change** 10-15%	....
☐	**Vaccum the Gravel**	....
☐	**Check Lighting**	....
☐	**Expiration dates** For Kits & Supplies	....

ADDITIONAL NOTES

Tank:		Days/Weeks Since the Last Test:
Date:	Fish count:	Fish Lost since the Last Count:
Fish Behavior:		Feeding:

Tick Box	Maintenance Check List	Maintenance check details
☐	**Filters Check**	
☐	**Pumps Check**	
☐	**Water Level**	
☐	**Water Temperature**	
☐	**Tubing Check**	
☐	**PH Level**	
☐	**Ammonia**	
☐	**Nitrite Level**	
☐	**Nitrate Level**	
☐	**Phosphate Level**	
☐	**Carbonate Hardness**	
☐	**Salinity Level**	
☐	**Calcium Level**	
☐	**Water Change** 10-15%	
☐	**Vaccum the Gravel**	
☐	**Check Lighting**	
☐	**Expiration dates** For Kits & Supplies	

ADDITIONAL NOTES

	Tank:		Days/Weeks Since the Last Test:

	Date:		Fish count:		Fish Lost since the Last Count:

	Fish Behavior:		Feeding:

Tick Box	Maintenance Check List	Maintenance check details
☐	**Filters Check**	
☐	**Pumps Check**	
☐	**Water Level**	
☐	**Water Temperature**	
☐	**Tubing Check**	
☐	**PH Level**	
☐	**Ammonia**	
☐	**Nitrite Level**	
☐	**Nitrate Level**	
☐	**Phosphate Level**	
☐	**Carbonate Hardness**	
☐	**Salinity Level**	
☐	**Calcium Level**	
☐	**Water Change** 10-15%	
☐	**Vaccum the Gravel**	
☐	**Check Lighting**	
☐	**Expiration dates** For Kits & Supplies	

ADDITIONAL NOTES

	Tank:		Days/Weeks Since the Last Test:
	Date:	Fish count:	Fish Lost since the Last Count:
	Fish Behavior:		Feeding:

Tick Box	Maintenance Check List	Maintenance check details
☐	**Filters Check**	
☐	**Pumps Check**	
☐	**Water Level**	
☐	**Water Temperature**	
☐	**Tubing Check**	
☐	**PH Level**	
☐	**Ammonia**	
☐	**Nitrite Level**	
☐	**Nitrate Level**	
☐	**Phosphate Level**	
☐	**Carbonate Hardness**	
☐	**Salinity Level**	
☐	**Calcium Level**	
☐	**Water Change** 10-15%	
☐	**Vaccum the Gravel**	
☐	**Check Lighting**	
☐	**Expiration dates** For Kits & Supplies	

ADDITIONAL NOTES

	Tank:			Days/Weeks Since the Last Test:

	Date:		Fish count:		Fish Lost since the Last Count:

	Fish Behavior:		Feeding:

Tick Box	Maintenance Check List	Maintenance check details
☐	**Filters Check**	....
☐	**Pumps Check**	....
☐	**Water Level**	....
☐	**Water Temperature**	....
☐	**Tubing Check**	....
☐	**PH Level**	....
☐	**Ammonia**	....
☐	**Nitrite Level**	....
☐	**Nitrate Level**	....
☐	**Phosphate Level**	....
☐	**Carbonate Hardness**	....
☐	**Salinity Level**	....
☐	**Calcium Level**	....
☐	**Water Change** 10-15%	....
☐	**Vaccum the Gravel**	....
☐	**Check Lighting**	....
☐	**Expiration dates** For Kits & Supplies	....

ADDITIONAL NOTES

	Tank:		Days/Weeks Since the Last Test:

| | Date: | | Fish count: | | Fish Lost since the Last Count: |

| | Fish Behavior: | | Feeding: |

Tick Box	Maintenance Check List	Maintenance check details
☐	**Filters Check**	
☐	**Pumps Check**	
☐	**Water Level**	
☐	**Water Temperature**	
☐	**Tubing Check**	
☐	**PH Level**	
☐	**Ammonia**	
☐	**Nitrite Level**	
☐	**Nitrate Level**	
☐	**Phosphate Level**	
☐	**Carbonate Hardness**	
☐	**Salinity Level**	
☐	**Calcium Level**	
☐	**Water Change** 10-15%	
☐	**Vaccum the Gravel**	
☐	**Check Lighting**	
☐	**Expiration dates** For Kits & Supplies	

ADDITIONAL NOTES

	Tank:			Days/Weeks Since the Last Test:
	Date:		Fish count:	Fish Lost since the Last Count:
	Fish Behavior:			Feeding:

Tick Box	Maintenance Check List	Maintenance check details
☐	**Filters Check**	....
☐	**Pumps Check**	....
☐	**Water Level**	....
☐	**Water Temperature**	....
☐	**Tubing Check**	....
☐	**PH Level**	....
☐	**Ammonia**	....
☐	**Nitrite Level**	....
☐	**Nitrate Level**	....
☐	**Phosphate Level**	....
☐	**Carbonate Hardness**	....
☐	**Salinity Level**	....
☐	**Calcium Level**	....
☐	**Water Change** 10-15%	....
☐	**Vaccum the Gravel**	....
☐	**Check Lighting**	....
☐	**Expiration dates** For Kits & Supplies	....

ADDITIONAL NOTES

Tank:	Days/Weeks Since the Last Test:

Date:	Fish count:

Fish Lost since the Last Count:

Fish Behavior:	Feeding:

Tick Box	Maintenance Check List	Maintenance check details
☐	**Filters Check**	
☐	**Pumps Check**	
☐	**Water Level**	
☐	**Water Temperature**	
☐	**Tubing Check**	
☐	**PH Level**	
☐	**Ammonia**	
☐	**Nitrite Level**	
☐	**Nitrate Level**	
☐	**Phosphate Level**	
☐	**Carbonate Hardness**	
☐	**Salinity Level**	
☐	**Calcium Level**	
☐	**Water Change** 10-15%	
☐	**Vaccum the Gravel**	
☐	**Check Lighting**	
☐	**Expiration dates** For Kits & Supplies	

ADDITIONAL NOTES

Tank:		Days/Weeks Since the Last Test:
Date:	Fish count:	Fish Lost since the Last Count:
Fish Behavior:		Feeding:

Tick Box	Maintenance Check List	Maintenance check details
☐	**Filters Check**	....
☐	**Pumps Check**	....
☐	**Water Level**	....
☐	**Water Temperature**	....
☐	**Tubing Check**	....
☐	**PH Level**	....
☐	**Ammonia**	....
☐	**Nitrite Level**	....
☐	**Nitrate Level**	....
☐	**Phosphate Level**	....
☐	**Carbonate Hardness**	....
☐	**Salinity Level**	....
☐	**Calcium Level**	....
☐	**Water Change** 10-15%	....
☐	**Vaccum the Gravel**	....
☐	**Check Lighting**	....
☐	**Expiration dates** For Kits & Supplies	....

ADDITIONAL NOTES

Tank:		Days/Weeks Since the Last Test:
Date:	Fish count:	Fish Lost since the Last Count:
Fish Behavior:		Feeding:

Tick Box	Maintenance Check List	Maintenance check details
☐	**Filters Check**	
☐	**Pumps Check**	
☐	**Water Level**	
☐	**Water Temperature**	
☐	**Tubing Check**	
☐	**PH Level**	
☐	**Ammonia**	
☐	**Nitrite Level**	
☐	**Nitrate Level**	
☐	**Phosphate Level**	
☐	**Carbonate Hardness**	
☐	**Salinity Level**	
☐	**Calcium Level**	
☐	**Water Change** 10-15%	
☐	**Vaccum the Gravel**	
☐	**Check Lighting**	
☐	**Expiration dates** For Kits & Supplies	

ADDITIONAL NOTES

	Tank:		Days/Weeks Since the Last Test:
	Date:	Fish count:	Fish Lost since the Last Count:
	Fish Behavior:		Feeding:

Tick Box	Maintenance Check List	Maintenance check details
☐	**Filters Check**	....
☐	**Pumps Check**	....
☐	**Water Level**	....
☐	**Water Temperature**	....
☐	**Tubing Check**	....
☐	**PH Level**	....
☐	**Ammonia**	....
☐	**Nitrite Level**	....
☐	**Nitrate Level**	....
☐	**Phosphate Level**	....
☐	**Carbonate Hardness**	....
☐	**Salinity Level**	....
☐	**Calcium Level**	....
☐	**Water Change** 10-15%	....
☐	**Vaccum the Gravel**	....
☐	**Check Lighting**	....
☐	**Expiration dates** For Kits & Supplies	....

ADDITIONAL NOTES

	Tank:		Days/Weeks Since the Last Test:
	Date:	Fish count:	Fish Lost since the Last Count:
	Fish Behavior:		Feeding:

Tick Box	Maintenance Check List	Maintenance check details
☐	**Filters Check**	
☐	**Pumps Check**	
☐	**Water Level**	
☐	**Water Temperature**	
☐	**Tubing Check**	
☐	**PH Level**	
☐	**Ammonia**	
☐	**Nitrite Level**	
☐	**Nitrate Level**	
☐	**Phosphate Level**	
☐	**Carbonate Hardness**	
☐	**Salinity Level**	
☐	**Calcium Level**	
☐	**Water Change** 10-15%	
☐	**Vaccum the Gravel**	
☐	**Check Lighting**	
☐	**Expiration dates** For Kits & Supplies	

ADDITIONAL NOTES

	Tank:		Days/Weeks Since the Last Test:
	Date:	Fish count:	Fish Lost since the Last Count:
	Fish Behavior:		Feeding:

Tick Box	Maintenance Check List	Maintenance check details
☐	**Filters Check**	
☐	**Pumps Check**	
☐	**Water Level**	
☐	**Water Temperature**	
☐	**Tubing Check**	
☐	**PH Level**	
☐	**Ammonia**	
☐	**Nitrite Level**	
☐	**Nitrate Level**	
☐	**Phosphate Level**	
☐	**Carbonate Hardness**	
☐	**Salinity Level**	
☐	**Calcium Level**	
☐	**Water Change** 10-15%	
☐	**Vaccum the Gravel**	
☐	**Check Lighting**	
☐	**Expiration dates** For Kits & Supplies	

ADDITIONAL NOTES

Tank:	Days/Weeks Since the Last Test:

Date:	Fish count:	Fish Lost since the Last Count:

Fish Behavior:	Feeding:

Tick Box	Maintenance Check List	Maintenance check details
☐	**Filters Check**	
☐	**Pumps Check**	
☐	**Water Level**	
☐	**Water Temperature**	
☐	**Tubing Check**	
☐	**PH Level**	
☐	**Ammonia**	
☐	**Nitrite Level**	
☐	**Nitrate Level**	
☐	**Phosphate Level**	
☐	**Carbonate Hardness**	
☐	**Salinity Level**	
☐	**Calcium Level**	
☐	**Water Change** 10-15%	
☐	**Vaccum the Gravel**	
☐	**Check Lighting**	
☐	**Expiration dates** For Kits & Supplies	

ADDITIONAL NOTES

Tank:		Days/Weeks Since the Last Test:

Date:	Fish count:	Fish Lost since the Last Count:

Fish Behavior:		Feeding:

Tick Box	Maintenance Check List	Maintenance check details
☐	**Filters Check**	
☐	**Pumps Check**	
☐	**Water Level**	
☐	**Water Temperature**	
☐	**Tubing Check**	
☐	**PH Level**	
☐	**Ammonia**	
☐	**Nitrite Level**	
☐	**Nitrate Level**	
☐	**Phosphate Level**	
☐	**Carbonate Hardness**	
☐	**Salinity Level**	
☐	**Calcium Level**	
☐	**Water Change** 10-15%	
☐	**Vaccum the Gravel**	
☐	**Check Lighting**	
☐	**Expiration dates** For Kits & Supplies	

ADDITIONAL NOTES

Tank:	Days/Weeks Since the Last Test:
Date:	Fish count:	Fish Lost since the Last Count:
Fish Behavior:	Feeding:

Tick Box	Maintenance Check List	Maintenance check details
☐	**Filters Check**	
☐	**Pumps Check**	
☐	**Water Level**	
☐	**Water Temperature**	
☐	**Tubing Check**	
☐	**PH Level**	
☐	**Ammonia**	
☐	**Nitrite Level**	
☐	**Nitrate Level**	
☐	**Phosphate Level**	
☐	**Carbonate Hardness**	
☐	**Salinity Level**	
☐	**Calcium Level**	
☐	**Water Change** 10-15%	
☐	**Vaccum the Gravel**	
☐	**Check Lighting**	
☐	**Expiration dates** For Kits & Supplies	

ADDITIONAL NOTES

	Tank:			Days/Weeks Since the Last Test:

Date: | Fish count:

Fish Behavior: | Fish Lost since the Last Count:

Feeding:

Tick Box	Maintenance Check List	Maintenance check details
☐	**Filters Check**	
☐	**Pumps Check**	
☐	**Water Level**	
☐	**Water Temperature**	
☐	**Tubing Check**	
☐	**PH Level**	
☐	**Ammonia**	
☐	**Nitrite Level**	
☐	**Nitrate Level**	
☐	**Phosphate Level**	
☐	**Carbonate Hardness**	
☐	**Salinity Level**	
☐	**Calcium Level**	
☐	**Water Change** 10-15%	
☐	**Vaccum the Gravel**	
☐	**Check Lighting**	
☐	**Expiration dates** For Kits & Supplies	

ADDITIONAL NOTES

	Tank:		Days/Weeks Since the Last Test:
Date:		Fish count:	Fish Lost since the Last Count:
Fish Behavior:			Feeding:

Tick Box	Maintenance Check List	Maintenance check details
☐	**Filters Check**	
☐	**Pumps Check**	
☐	**Water Level**	
☐	**Water Temperature**	
☐	**Tubing Check**	
☐	**PH Level**	
☐	**Ammonia**	
☐	**Nitrite Level**	
☐	**Nitrate Level**	
☐	**Phosphate Level**	
☐	**Carbonate Hardness**	
☐	**Salinity Level**	
☐	**Calcium Level**	
☐	**Water Change** 10-15%	
☐	**Vaccum the Gravel**	
☐	**Check Lighting**	
☐	**Expiration dates** For Kits & Supplies	

ADDITIONAL NOTES

	Tank:			Days/Weeks Since the Last Test:
	Date:	Fish count:		Fish Lost since the Last Count:
	Fish Behavior:			Feeding:

Tick Box	Maintenance Check List	Maintenance check details
☐	**Filters Check**	....
☐	**Pumps Check**	....
☐	**Water Level**	....
☐	**Water Temperature**	....
☐	**Tubing Check**	....
☐	**PH Level**	....
☐	**Ammonia**	....
☐	**Nitrite Level**	....
☐	**Nitrate Level**	....
☐	**Phosphate Level**	....
☐	**Carbonate Hardness**	....
☐	**Salinity Level**	....
☐	**Calcium Level**	....
☐	**Water Change** 10-15%	....
☐	**Vaccum the Gravel**	....
☐	**Check Lighting**	....
☐	**Expiration dates** For Kits & Supplies	....

ADDITIONAL NOTES

Tank:		Days/Weeks Since the Last Test:
Date:	Fish count:	Fish Lost since the Last Count:
Fish Behavior:		Feeding:

Tick Box	Maintenance Check List	Maintenance check details
☐	**Filters Check**	
☐	**Pumps Check**	
☐	**Water Level**	
☐	**Water Temperature**	
☐	**Tubing Check**	
☐	**PH Level**	
☐	**Ammonia**	
☐	**Nitrite Level**	
☐	**Nitrate Level**	
☐	**Phosphate Level**	
☐	**Carbonate Hardness**	
☐	**Salinity Level**	
☐	**Calcium Level**	
☐	**Water Change** 10-15%	
☐	**Vaccum the Gravel**	
☐	**Check Lighting**	
☐	**Expiration dates** For Kits & Supplies	

ADDITIONAL NOTES

	Tank:			Days/Weeks Since the Last Test:
	Date:		Fish count:	Fish Lost since the Last Count:
	Fish Behavior:			Feeding:

Tick Box	Maintenance Check List	Maintenance check details
☐	**Filters Check**	
☐	**Pumps Check**	
☐	**Water Level**	
☐	**Water Temperature**	
☐	**Tubing Check**	
☐	**PH Level**	
☐	**Ammonia**	
☐	**Nitrite Level**	
☐	**Nitrate Level**	
☐	**Phosphate Level**	
☐	**Carbonate Hardness**	
☐	**Salinity Level**	
☐	**Calcium Level**	
☐	**Water Change** 10-15%	
☐	**Vaccum the Gravel**	
☐	**Check Lighting**	
☐	**Expiration dates** For Kits & Supplies	

ADDITIONAL NOTES

	Tank:			Days/Weeks Since the Last Test:
	Date:	Fish count:		Fish Lost since the Last Count:
	Fish Behavior:			Feeding:

Tick Box	Maintenance Check List	Maintenance check details
☐	**Filters Check**	
☐	**Pumps Check**	
☐	**Water Level**	
☐	**Water Temperature**	
☐	**Tubing Check**	
☐	**PH Level**	
☐	**Ammonia**	
☐	**Nitrite Level**	
☐	**Nitrate Level**	
☐	**Phosphate Level**	
☐	**Carbonate Hardness**	
☐	**Salinity Level**	
☐	**Calcium Level**	
☐	**Water Change** 10-15%	
☐	**Vaccum the Gravel**	
☐	**Check Lighting**	
☐	**Expiration dates** For Kits & Supplies	

ADDITIONAL NOTES

	Tank:		Days/Weeks Since the Last Test:
	Date:	Fish count:	Fish Lost since the Last Count:
	Fish Behavior:		Feeding:

Tick Box	Maintenance Check List	Maintenance check details
☐	**Filters Check**	....
☐	**Pumps Check**	....
☐	**Water Level**	....
☐	**Water Temperature**	....
☐	**Tubing Check**	....
☐	**PH Level**	....
☐	**Ammonia**	....
☐	**Nitrite Level**	....
☐	**Nitrate Level**	....
☐	**Phosphate Level**	....
☐	**Carbonate Hardness**	....
☐	**Salinity Level**	....
☐	**Calcium Level**	....
☐	**Water Change** 10-15%	....
☐	**Vaccum the Gravel**	....
☐	**Check Lighting**	....
☐	**Expiration dates** For Kits & Supplies	....

ADDITIONAL NOTES

	Tank:		Days/Weeks Since the Last Test:

	Date:		Fish count:		Fish Lost since the Last Count:

	Fish Behavior:		Feeding:

Tick Box	Maintenance Check List	Maintenance check details
☐	**Filters Check**	
☐	**Pumps Check**	
☐	**Water Level**	
☐	**Water Temperature**	
☐	**Tubing Check**	
☐	**PH Level**	
☐	**Ammonia**	
☐	**Nitrite Level**	
☐	**Nitrate Level**	
☐	**Phosphate Level**	
☐	**Carbonate Hardness**	
☐	**Salinity Level**	
☐	**Calcium Level**	
☐	**Water Change** 10-15%	
☐	**Vaccum the Gravel**	
☐	**Check Lighting**	
☐	**Expiration dates** For Kits & Supplies	

ADDITIONAL NOTES

	Tank:		Days/Weeks Since the Last Test:
Date:		Fish count:	Fish Lost since the Last Count:
Fish Behavior:			Feeding:

Tick Box	Maintenance Check List	Maintenance check details
☐	**Filters Check**	
☐	**Pumps Check**	
☐	**Water Level**	
☐	**Water Temperature**	
☐	**Tubing Check**	
☐	**PH Level**	
☐	**Ammonia**	
☐	**Nitrite Level**	
☐	**Nitrate Level**	
☐	**Phosphate Level**	
☐	**Carbonate Hardness**	
☐	**Salinity Level**	
☐	**Calcium Level**	
☐	**Water Change** 10-15%	
☐	**Vaccum the Gravel**	
☐	**Check Lighting**	
☐	**Expiration dates** For Kits & Supplies	

ADDITIONAL NOTES

Tank:	Days/Weeks Since the Last Test:
Date:	Fish count:	Fish Lost since the Last Count:
Fish Behavior:	Feeding:

Tick Box	Maintenance Check List	Maintenance check details
☐	**Filters Check**	
☐	**Pumps Check**	
☐	**Water Level**	
☐	**Water Temperature**	
☐	**Tubing Check**	
☐	**PH Level**	
☐	**Ammonia**	
☐	**Nitrite Level**	
☐	**Nitrate Level**	
☐	**Phosphate Level**	
☐	**Carbonate Hardness**	
☐	**Salinity Level**	
☐	**Calcium Level**	
☐	**Water Change** 10-15%	
☐	**Vaccum the Gravel**	
☐	**Check Lighting**	
☐	**Expiration dates** For Kits & Supplies	

ADDITIONAL NOTES

Tank:		Days/Weeks Since the Last Test:
Date:	Fish count:	Fish Lost since the Last Count:
Fish Behavior:		Feeding:

Tick Box	Maintenance Check List	Maintenance check details
☐	**Filters Check**	
☐	**Pumps Check**	
☐	**Water Level**	
☐	**Water Temperature**	
☐	**Tubing Check**	
☐	**PH Level**	
☐	**Ammonia**	
☐	**Nitrite Level**	
☐	**Nitrate Level**	
☐	**Phosphate Level**	
☐	**Carbonate Hardness**	
☐	**Salinity Level**	
☐	**Calcium Level**	
☐	**Water Change** 10-15%	
☐	**Vaccum the Gravel**	
☐	**Check Lighting**	
☐	**Expiration dates** For Kits & Supplies	

ADDITIONAL NOTES

Tank:	Days/Weeks Since the Last Test:
Date:	Fish count:	Fish Lost since the Last Count:
Fish Behavior:	Feeding:

Tick Box	Maintenance Check List	Maintenance check details
☐	**Filters Check**	
☐	**Pumps Check**	
☐	**Water Level**	
☐	**Water Temperature**	
☐	**Tubing Check**	
☐	**PH Level**	
☐	**Ammonia**	
☐	**Nitrite Level**	
☐	**Nitrate Level**	
☐	**Phosphate Level**	
☐	**Carbonate Hardness**	
☐	**Salinity Level**	
☐	**Calcium Level**	
☐	**Water Change** 10-15%	
☐	**Vaccum the Gravel**	
☐	**Check Lighting**	
☐	**Expiration dates** For Kits & Supplies	

ADDITIONAL NOTES

	Tank:		Days/Weeks Since the Last Test:
	Date:	Fish count:	Fish Lost since the Last Count:
	Fish Behavior:		Feeding:

Tick Box	Maintenance Check List	Maintenance check details
☐	**Filters Check**	
☐	**Pumps Check**	
☐	**Water Level**	
☐	**Water Temperature**	
☐	**Tubing Check**	
☐	**PH Level**	
☐	**Ammonia**	
☐	**Nitrite Level**	
☐	**Nitrate Level**	
☐	**Phosphate Level**	
☐	**Carbonate Hardness**	
☐	**Salinity Level**	
☐	**Calcium Level**	
☐	**Water Change** 10-15%	
☐	**Vaccum the Gravel**	
☐	**Check Lighting**	
☐	**Expiration dates** For Kits & Supplies	

ADDITIONAL NOTES

Tank:		Days/Weeks Since the Last Test:
Date:	Fish count:	Fish Lost since the Last Count:
Fish Behavior:		Feeding:

Tick Box	Maintenance Check List	Maintenance check details
☐	**Filters Check**	
☐	**Pumps Check**	
☐	**Water Level**	
☐	**Water Temperature**	
☐	**Tubing Check**	
☐	**PH Level**	
☐	**Ammonia**	
☐	**Nitrite Level**	
☐	**Nitrate Level**	
☐	**Phosphate Level**	
☐	**Carbonate Hardness**	
☐	**Salinity Level**	
☐	**Calcium Level**	
☐	**Water Change** 10-15%	
☐	**Vaccum the Gravel**	
☐	**Check Lighting**	
☐	**Expiration dates** For Kits & Supplies	

ADDITIONAL NOTES

🐟 Tank:		📅 Days/Weeks Since the Last Test:
📅 Date:	🐟 Fish count:	🐟 Fish Lost since the Last Count:
🌵 Fish Behavior:		🐟 Feeding:

Tick Box	Maintenance Check List	Maintenance check details
☐	**Filters Check**	
☐	**Pumps Check**	
☐	**Water Level**	
☐	**Water Temperature**	
☐	**Tubing Check**	
☐	**PH Level**	
☐	**Ammonia**	
☐	**Nitrite Level**	
☐	**Nitrate Level**	
☐	**Phosphate Level**	
☐	**Carbonate Hardness**	
☐	**Salinity Level**	
☐	**Calcium Level**	
☐	**Water Change** 10-15%	
☐	**Vaccum the Gravel**	
☐	**Check Lighting**	
☐	**Expiration dates** For Kits & Supplies	

ADDITIONAL NOTES

	Tank:		Days/Weeks Since the Last Test:
	Date:	Fish count:	Fish Lost since the Last Count:
	Fish Behavior:		Feeding:

Tick Box	Maintenance Check List	Maintenance check details
☐	**Filters Check**	
☐	**Pumps Check**	
☐	**Water Level**	
☐	**Water Temperature**	
☐	**Tubing Check**	
☐	**PH Level**	
☐	**Ammonia**	
☐	**Nitrite Level**	
☐	**Nitrate Level**	
☐	**Phosphate Level**	
☐	**Carbonate Hardness**	
☐	**Salinity Level**	
☐	**Calcium Level**	
☐	**Water Change** 10-15%	
☐	**Vaccum the Gravel**	
☐	**Check Lighting**	
☐	**Expiration dates** For Kits & Supplies	

ADDITIONAL NOTES

| Tank: | Days/Weeks Since the Last Test: |

| Date: | Fish count: | Fish Lost since the Last Count: |

| Fish Behavior: | Feeding: |

Tick Box	Maintenance Check List	Maintenance check details
☐	**Filters Check**	....
☐	**Pumps Check**	....
☐	**Water Level**	....
☐	**Water Temperature**	....
☐	**Tubing Check**	....
☐	**PH Level**	....
☐	**Ammonia**	....
☐	**Nitrite Level**	....
☐	**Nitrate Level**	....
☐	**Phosphate Level**	....
☐	**Carbonate Hardness**	....
☐	**Salinity Level**	....
☐	**Calcium Level**	....
☐	**Water Change** 10-15%	....
☐	**Vaccum the Gravel**	....
☐	**Check Lighting**	....
☐	**Expiration dates** For Kits & Supplies	....

ADDITIONAL NOTES

Tank:	Days/Weeks Since the Last Test:
Date:	Fish count:
Fish Behavior:	Fish Lost since the Last Count:
	Feeding:

Tick Box	Maintenance Check List	Maintenance check details
☐	Filters Check	
☐	Pumps Check	
☐	Water Level	
☐	Water Temperature	
☐	Tubing Check	
☐	PH Level	
☐	Ammonia	
☐	Nitrite Level	
☐	Nitrate Level	
☐	Phosphate Level	
☐	Carbonate Hardness	
☐	Salinity Level	
☐	Calcium Level	
☐	Water Change 10-15%	
☐	Vaccum the Gravel	
☐	Check Lighting	
☐	Expiration dates For Kits & Supplies	

ADDITIONAL NOTES

	Tank:		Days/Weeks Since the Last Test:
	Date:	Fish count:	Fish Lost since the Last Count:
	Fish Behavior:		Feeding:

Tick Box	Maintenance Check List	Maintenance check details
☐	**Filters Check**	
☐	**Pumps Check**	
☐	**Water Level**	
☐	**Water Temperature**	
☐	**Tubing Check**	
☐	**PH Level**	
☐	**Ammonia**	
☐	**Nitrite Level**	
☐	**Nitrate Level**	
☐	**Phosphate Level**	
☐	**Carbonate Hardness**	
☐	**Salinity Level**	
☐	**Calcium Level**	
☐	**Water Change** 10-15%	
☐	**Vaccum the Gravel**	
☐	**Check Lighting**	
☐	**Expiration dates** For Kits & Supplies	

ADDITIONAL NOTES

Tank:		Days/Weeks Since the Last Test:
Date:	Fish count:	Fish Lost since the Last Count:
Fish Behavior:		Feeding:

Tick Box	Maintenance Check List	Maintenance check details
☐	**Filters Check**	
☐	**Pumps Check**	
☐	**Water Level**	
☐	**Water Temperature**	
☐	**Tubing Check**	
☐	**PH Level**	
☐	**Ammonia**	
☐	**Nitrite Level**	
☐	**Nitrate Level**	
☐	**Phosphate Level**	
☐	**Carbonate Hardness**	
☐	**Salinity Level**	
☐	**Calcium Level**	
☐	**Water Change** 10-15%	
☐	**Vaccum the Gravel**	
☐	**Check Lighting**	
☐	**Expiration dates** For Kits & Supplies	

ADDITIONAL NOTES

	Tank:			Days/Weeks Since the Last Test:

Tank:

Days/Weeks Since the Last Test:

Date:

Fish count:

Fish Lost since the Last Count:

Fish Behavior:

Feeding:

Tick Box	Maintenance Check List	Maintenance check details
☐	**Filters Check**	
☐	**Pumps Check**	
☐	**Water Level**	
☐	**Water Temperature**	
☐	**Tubing Check**	
☐	**PH Level**	
☐	**Ammonia**	
☐	**Nitrite Level**	
☐	**Nitrate Level**	
☐	**Phosphate Level**	
☐	**Carbonate Hardness**	
☐	**Salinity Level**	
☐	**Calcium Level**	
☐	**Water Change** 10-15%	
☐	**Vaccum the Gravel**	
☐	**Check Lighting**	
☐	**Expiration dates** For Kits & Supplies	

ADDITIONAL NOTES

Tank:	Days/Weeks Since the Last Test:
Date:	Fish count:	Fish Lost since the Last Count:
Fish Behavior:	Feeding:

Tick Box	Maintenance Check List	Maintenance check details
☐	**Filters Check**	
☐	**Pumps Check**	
☐	**Water Level**	
☐	**Water Temperature**	
☐	**Tubing Check**	
☐	**PH Level**	
☐	**Ammonia**	
☐	**Nitrite Level**	
☐	**Nitrate Level**	
☐	**Phosphate Level**	
☐	**Carbonate Hardness**	
☐	**Salinity Level**	
☐	**Calcium Level**	
☐	**Water Change** 10-15%	
☐	**Vaccum the Gravel**	
☐	**Check Lighting**	
☐	**Expiration dates** For Kits & Supplies	

ADDITIONAL NOTES

	Tank:		Days/Weeks Since the Last Test:

	Date:		Fish count:		Fish Lost since the Last Count:

	Fish Behavior:		Feeding:

Tick Box	Maintenance Check List	Maintenance check details
☐	**Filters Check**	
☐	**Pumps Check**	
☐	**Water Level**	
☐	**Water Temperature**	
☐	**Tubing Check**	
☐	**PH Level**	
☐	**Ammonia**	
☐	**Nitrite Level**	
☐	**Nitrate Level**	
☐	**Phosphate Level**	
☐	**Carbonate Hardness**	
☐	**Salinity Level**	
☐	**Calcium Level**	
☐	**Water Change** 10-15%	
☐	**Vaccum the Gravel**	
☐	**Check Lighting**	
☐	**Expiration dates** For Kits & Supplies	

ADDITIONAL NOTES

	Tank:		Days/Weeks Since the Last Test:

	Date:		Fish count:		Fish Lost since the Last Count:

	Fish Behavior:		Feeding:

Tick Box	Maintenance Check List	Maintenance check details
☐	**Filters Check**	
☐	**Pumps Check**	
☐	**Water Level**	
☐	**Water Temperature**	
☐	**Tubing Check**	
☐	**PH Level**	
☐	**Ammonia**	
☐	**Nitrite Level**	
☐	**Nitrate Level**	
☐	**Phosphate Level**	
☐	**Carbonate Hardness**	
☐	**Salinity Level**	
☐	**Calcium Level**	
☐	**Water Change** 10-15%	
☐	**Vaccum the Gravel**	
☐	**Check Lighting**	
☐	**Expiration dates** For Kits & Supplies	

ADDITIONAL NOTES

	Tank:		Days/Weeks Since the Last Test:
	Date:	Fish count:	Fish Lost since the Last Count:
	Fish Behavior:		Feeding:

Tick Box	Maintenance Check List	Maintenance check details
☐	**Filters Check**	
☐	**Pumps Check**	
☐	**Water Level**	
☐	**Water Temperature**	
☐	**Tubing Check**	
☐	**PH Level**	
☐	**Ammonia**	
☐	**Nitrite Level**	
☐	**Nitrate Level**	
☐	**Phosphate Level**	
☐	**Carbonate Hardness**	
☐	**Salinity Level**	
☐	**Calcium Level**	
☐	**Water Change** 10-15%	
☐	**Vaccum the Gravel**	
☐	**Check Lighting**	
☐	**Expiration dates** For Kits & Supplies	

ADDITIONAL NOTES

	Tank:				Days/Weeks Since the Last Test:
	Date:		Fish count:		Fish Lost since the Last Count:
	Fish Behavior:				Feeding:

Tick Box	Maintenance Check List	Maintenance check details
☐	**Filters Check**	
☐	**Pumps Check**	
☐	**Water Level**	
☐	**Water Temperature**	
☐	**Tubing Check**	
☐	**PH Level**	
☐	**Ammonia**	
☐	**Nitrite Level**	
☐	**Nitrate Level**	
☐	**Phosphate Level**	
☐	**Carbonate Hardness**	
☐	**Salinity Level**	
☐	**Calcium Level**	
☐	**Water Change** 10-15%	
☐	**Vaccum the Gravel**	
☐	**Check Lighting**	
☐	**Expiration dates** For Kits & Supplies	

ADDITIONAL NOTES

| Tank: | Days/Weeks Since the Last Test: |

| Date: | Fish count: | Fish Lost since the Last Count: |

| Fish Behavior: | Feeding: |

Tick Box	Maintenance Check List	Maintenance check details
☐	**Filters Check**	
☐	**Pumps Check**	
☐	**Water Level**	
☐	**Water Temperature**	
☐	**Tubing Check**	
☐	**PH Level**	
☐	**Ammonia**	
☐	**Nitrite Level**	
☐	**Nitrate Level**	
☐	**Phosphate Level**	
☐	**Carbonate Hardness**	
☐	**Salinity Level**	
☐	**Calcium Level**	
☐	**Water Change** 10-15%	
☐	**Vaccum the Gravel**	
☐	**Check Lighting**	
☐	**Expiration dates** For Kits & Supplies	

ADDITIONAL NOTES

	Tank:		Days/Weeks Since the Last Test:
	Date:	Fish count:	Fish Lost since the Last Count:
	Fish Behavior:		Feeding:

Tick Box	Maintenance Check List	Maintenance check details
☐	**Filters Check**	....
☐	**Pumps Check**	....
☐	**Water Level**	....
☐	**Water Temperature**	....
☐	**Tubing Check**	....
☐	**PH Level**	....
☐	**Ammonia**	....
☐	**Nitrite Level**	....
☐	**Nitrate Level**	....
☐	**Phosphate Level**	....
☐	**Carbonate Hardness**	....
☐	**Salinity Level**	....
☐	**Calcium Level**	....
☐	**Water Change** 10-15%	....
☐	**Vaccum the Gravel**	....
☐	**Check Lighting**	....
☐	**Expiration dates** For Kits & Supplies	....

ADDITIONAL NOTES

	Tank:		Days/Weeks Since the Last Test:
	Date:	Fish count:	Fish Lost since the Last Count:
	Fish Behavior:		Feeding:

Tick Box	Maintenance Check List	Maintenance check details
☐	**Filters Check**	
☐	**Pumps Check**	
☐	**Water Level**	
☐	**Water Temperature**	
☐	**Tubing Check**	
☐	**PH Level**	
☐	**Ammonia**	
☐	**Nitrite Level**	
☐	**Nitrate Level**	
☐	**Phosphate Level**	
☐	**Carbonate Hardness**	
☐	**Salinity Level**	
☐	**Calcium Level**	
☐	**Water Change** 10-15%	
☐	**Vaccum the Gravel**	
☐	**Check Lighting**	
☐	**Expiration dates** For Kits & Supplies	

ADDITIONAL NOTES

Tank:		Days/Weeks Since the Last Test:
Date:	Fish count:	Fish Lost since the Last Count:
Fish Behavior:		Feeding:

Tick Box	Maintenance Check List	Maintenance check details
☐	**Filters Check**	
☐	**Pumps Check**	
☐	**Water Level**	
☐	**Water Temperature**	
☐	**Tubing Check**	
☐	**PH Level**	
☐	**Ammonia**	
☐	**Nitrite Level**	
☐	**Nitrate Level**	
☐	**Phosphate Level**	
☐	**Carbonate Hardness**	
☐	**Salinity Level**	
☐	**Calcium Level**	
☐	**Water Change** 10-15%	
☐	**Vaccum the Gravel**	
☐	**Check Lighting**	
☐	**Expiration dates** For Kits & Supplies	

ADDITIONAL NOTES

Tank:		Days/Weeks Since the Last Test:
Date:	Fish count:	Fish Lost since the Last Count:
Fish Behavior:		Feeding:

Tick Box	Maintenance Check List	Maintenance check details
☐	**Filters Check**	
☐	**Pumps Check**	
☐	**Water Level**	
☐	**Water Temperature**	
☐	**Tubing Check**	
☐	**PH Level**	
☐	**Ammonia**	
☐	**Nitrite Level**	
☐	**Nitrate Level**	
☐	**Phosphate Level**	
☐	**Carbonate Hardness**	
☐	**Salinity Level**	
☐	**Calcium Level**	
☐	**Water Change** 10-15%	
☐	**Vaccum the Gravel**	
☐	**Check Lighting**	
☐	**Expiration dates** For Kits & Supplies	

ADDITIONAL NOTES

Tank:		Days/Weeks Since the Last Test:
Date:	Fish count:	Fish Lost since the Last Count:
Fish Behavior:		Feeding:

Tick Box	Maintenance Check List	Maintenance check details
☐	**Filters Check**	
☐	**Pumps Check**	
☐	**Water Level**	
☐	**Water Temperature**	
☐	**Tubing Check**	
☐	**PH Level**	
☐	**Ammonia**	
☐	**Nitrite Level**	
☐	**Nitrate Level**	
☐	**Phosphate Level**	
☐	**Carbonate Hardness**	
☐	**Salinity Level**	
☐	**Calcium Level**	
☐	**Water Change** 10-15%	
☐	**Vaccum the Gravel**	
☐	**Check Lighting**	
☐	**Expiration dates** For Kits & Supplies	

ADDITIONAL NOTES

	Tank:			Days/Weeks Since the Last Test:

	Date:		Fish count:		Fish Lost since the Last Count:

	Fish Behavior:			Feeding:

Tick Box	Maintenance Check List	Maintenance check details
☐	**Filters Check**	
☐	**Pumps Check**	
☐	**Water Level**	
☐	**Water Temperature**	
☐	**Tubing Check**	
☐	**PH Level**	
☐	**Ammonia**	
☐	**Nitrite Level**	
☐	**Nitrate Level**	
☐	**Phosphate Level**	
☐	**Carbonate Hardness**	
☐	**Salinity Level**	
☐	**Calcium Level**	
☐	**Water Change** 10-15%	
☐	**Vaccum the Gravel**	
☐	**Check Lighting**	
☐	**Expiration dates** For Kits & Supplies	

ADDITIONAL NOTES

Tank:		Days/Weeks Since the Last Test:
Date:	Fish count:	Fish Lost since the Last Count:
Fish Behavior:		Feeding:

Tick Box	Maintenance Check List	Maintenance check details
☐	**Filters Check**	
☐	**Pumps Check**	
☐	**Water Level**	
☐	**Water Temperature**	
☐	**Tubing Check**	
☐	**PH Level**	
☐	**Ammonia**	
☐	**Nitrite Level**	
☐	**Nitrate Level**	
☐	**Phosphate Level**	
☐	**Carbonate Hardness**	
☐	**Salinity Level**	
☐	**Calcium Level**	
☐	**Water Change** 10-15%	
☐	**Vaccum the Gravel**	
☐	**Check Lighting**	
☐	**Expiration dates** For Kits & Supplies	

ADDITIONAL NOTES

Tank:		Days/Weeks Since the Last Test:
Date:	Fish count:	Fish Lost since the Last Count:
Fish Behavior:		Feeding:

Tick Box	Maintenance Check List	Maintenance check details
☐	**Filters Check**	
☐	**Pumps Check**	
☐	**Water Level**	
☐	**Water Temperature**	
☐	**Tubing Check**	
☐	**PH Level**	
☐	**Ammonia**	
☐	**Nitrite Level**	
☐	**Nitrate Level**	
☐	**Phosphate Level**	
☐	**Carbonate Hardness**	
☐	**Salinity Level**	
☐	**Calcium Level**	
☐	**Water Change** 10-15%	
☐	**Vaccum the Gravel**	
☐	**Check Lighting**	
☐	**Expiration dates** For Kits & Supplies	

ADDITIONAL NOTES

	Tank:		Days/Weeks Since the Last Test:
	Date:	Fish count:	Fish Lost since the Last Count:
	Fish Behavior:		Feeding:

Tick Box	Maintenance Check List	Maintenance check details
☐	**Filters Check**	
☐	**Pumps Check**	
☐	**Water Level**	
☐	**Water Temperature**	
☐	**Tubing Check**	
☐	**PH Level**	
☐	**Ammonia**	
☐	**Nitrite Level**	
☐	**Nitrate Level**	
☐	**Phosphate Level**	
☐	**Carbonate Hardness**	
☐	**Salinity Level**	
☐	**Calcium Level**	
☐	**Water Change** 10-15%	
☐	**Vaccum the Gravel**	
☐	**Check Lighting**	
☐	**Expiration dates** For Kits & Supplies	

ADDITIONAL NOTES

	Tank:		Days/Weeks Since the Last Test:

	Date:		Fish count:		Fish Lost since the Last Count:

	Fish Behavior:		Feeding:

Tick Box	Maintenance Check List	Maintenance check details
☐	**Filters Check**	
☐	**Pumps Check**	
☐	**Water Level**	
☐	**Water Temperature**	
☐	**Tubing Check**	
☐	**PH Level**	
☐	**Ammonia**	
☐	**Nitrite Level**	
☐	**Nitrate Level**	
☐	**Phosphate Level**	
☐	**Carbonate Hardness**	
☐	**Salinity Level**	
☐	**Calcium Level**	
☐	**Water Change** 10-15%	
☐	**Vaccum the Gravel**	
☐	**Check Lighting**	
☐	**Expiration dates** For Kits & Supplies	

ADDITIONAL NOTES

Tank:		Days/Weeks Since the Last Test:
Date:	Fish count:	Fish Lost since the Last Count:
Fish Behavior:		Feeding:

Tick Box	Maintenance Check List	Maintenance check details
☐	**Filters Check**	
☐	**Pumps Check**	
☐	**Water Level**	
☐	**Water Temperature**	
☐	**Tubing Check**	
☐	**PH Level**	
☐	**Ammonia**	
☐	**Nitrite Level**	
☐	**Nitrate Level**	
☐	**Phosphate Level**	
☐	**Carbonate Hardness**	
☐	**Salinity Level**	
☐	**Calcium Level**	
☐	**Water Change** 10-15%	
☐	**Vaccum the Gravel**	
☐	**Check Lighting**	
☐	**Expiration dates** For Kits & Supplies	

ADDITIONAL NOTES

	Tank:		Days/Weeks Since the Last Test:
	Date:	Fish count:	Fish Lost since the Last Count:
	Fish Behavior:		Feeding:

Tick Box	Maintenance Check List	Maintenance check details
☐	**Filters Check**	
☐	**Pumps Check**	
☐	**Water Level**	
☐	**Water Temperature**	
☐	**Tubing Check**	
☐	**PH Level**	
☐	**Ammonia**	
☐	**Nitrite Level**	
☐	**Nitrate Level**	
☐	**Phosphate Level**	
☐	**Carbonate Hardness**	
☐	**Salinity Level**	
☐	**Calcium Level**	
☐	**Water Change** 10-15%	
☐	**Vaccum the Gravel**	
☐	**Check Lighting**	
☐	**Expiration dates** For Kits & Supplies	

ADDITIONAL NOTES

	Tank:		Days/Weeks Since the Last Test:

	Date:		Fish count:		Fish Lost since the Last Count:

	Fish Behavior:		Feeding:

Tick Box	Maintenance Check List	Maintenance check details
☐	**Filters Check**	
☐	**Pumps Check**	
☐	**Water Level**	
☐	**Water Temperature**	
☐	**Tubing Check**	
☐	**PH Level**	
☐	**Ammonia**	
☐	**Nitrite Level**	
☐	**Nitrate Level**	
☐	**Phosphate Level**	
☐	**Carbonate Hardness**	
☐	**Salinity Level**	
☐	**Calcium Level**	
☐	**Water Change** 10-15%	
☐	**Vaccum the Gravel**	
☐	**Check Lighting**	
☐	**Expiration dates** For Kits & Supplies	

ADDITIONAL NOTES

	Tank:		Days/Weeks Since the Last Test:

Date:	Fish count:	Fish Lost since the Last Count:

Fish Behavior:		Feeding:

Tick Box	Maintenance Check List	Maintenance check details
☐	**Filters Check**	
☐	**Pumps Check**	
☐	**Water Level**	
☐	**Water Temperature**	
☐	**Tubing Check**	
☐	**PH Level**	
☐	**Ammonia**	
☐	**Nitrite Level**	
☐	**Nitrate Level**	
☐	**Phosphate Level**	
☐	**Carbonate Hardness**	
☐	**Salinity Level**	
☐	**Calcium Level**	
☐	**Water Change** 10-15%	
☐	**Vaccum the Gravel**	
☐	**Check Lighting**	
☐	**Expiration dates** For Kits & Supplies	

ADDITIONAL NOTES

Tank:		Days/Weeks Since the Last Test:
Date:	Fish count:	Fish Lost since the Last Count:
Fish Behavior:		Feeding:

Tick Box	Maintenance Check List	Maintenance check details
☐	**Filters Check**	
☐	**Pumps Check**	
☐	**Water Level**	
☐	**Water Temperature**	
☐	**Tubing Check**	
☐	**PH Level**	
☐	**Ammonia**	
☐	**Nitrite Level**	
☐	**Nitrate Level**	
☐	**Phosphate Level**	
☐	**Carbonate Hardness**	
☐	**Salinity Level**	
☐	**Calcium Level**	
☐	**Water Change** 10-15%	
☐	**Vaccum the Gravel**	
☐	**Check Lighting**	
☐	**Expiration dates** For Kits & Supplies	

ADDITIONAL NOTES

Tank:	Days/Weeks Since the Last Test:
Date:	Fish count:	Fish Lost since the Last Count:
Fish Behavior:	Feeding:

Tick Box	Maintenance Check List	Maintenance check details
☐	**Filters Check**	
☐	**Pumps Check**	
☐	**Water Level**	
☐	**Water Temperature**	
☐	**Tubing Check**	
☐	**PH Level**	
☐	**Ammonia**	
☐	**Nitrite Level**	
☐	**Nitrate Level**	
☐	**Phosphate Level**	
☐	**Carbonate Hardness**	
☐	**Salinity Level**	
☐	**Calcium Level**	
☐	**Water Change** 10-15%	
☐	**Vaccum the Gravel**	
☐	**Check Lighting**	
☐	**Expiration dates** For Kits & Supplies	

ADDITIONAL NOTES

	Tank:		Days/Weeks Since the Last Test:
	Date:	Fish count:	Fish Lost since the Last Count:
	Fish Behavior:		Feeding:

Tick Box	Maintenance Check List	Maintenance check details
☐	**Filters Check**	
☐	**Pumps Check**	
☐	**Water Level**	
☐	**Water Temperature**	
☐	**Tubing Check**	
☐	**PH Level**	
☐	**Ammonia**	
☐	**Nitrite Level**	
☐	**Nitrate Level**	
☐	**Phosphate Level**	
☐	**Carbonate Hardness**	
☐	**Salinity Level**	
☐	**Calcium Level**	
☐	**Water Change** 10-15%	
☐	**Vaccum the Gravel**	
☐	**Check Lighting**	
☐	**Expiration dates** For Kits & Supplies	

ADDITIONAL NOTES

	Tank:		Days/Weeks Since the Last Test:
	Date:	Fish count:	Fish Lost since the Last Count:
	Fish Behavior:		Feeding:

Tick Box	Maintenance Check List	Maintenance check details
☐	**Filters Check**	
☐	**Pumps Check**	
☐	**Water Level**	
☐	**Water Temperature**	
☐	**Tubing Check**	
☐	**PH Level**	
☐	**Ammonia**	
☐	**Nitrite Level**	
☐	**Nitrate Level**	
☐	**Phosphate Level**	
☐	**Carbonate Hardness**	
☐	**Salinity Level**	
☐	**Calcium Level**	
☐	**Water Change** 10-15%	
☐	**Vaccum the Gravel**	
☐	**Check Lighting**	
☐	**Expiration dates** For Kits & Supplies	

ADDITIONAL NOTES

	Tank:		Days/Weeks Since the Last Test:
	Date:	Fish count:	Fish Lost since the Last Count:
	Fish Behavior:		Feeding:

Tick Box	Maintenance Check List	Maintenance check details
☐	**Filters Check**	
☐	**Pumps Check**	
☐	**Water Level**	
☐	**Water Temperature**	
☐	**Tubing Check**	
☐	**PH Level**	
☐	**Ammonia**	
☐	**Nitrite Level**	
☐	**Nitrate Level**	
☐	**Phosphate Level**	
☐	**Carbonate Hardness**	
☐	**Salinity Level**	
☐	**Calcium Level**	
☐	**Water Change** 10-15%	
☐	**Vaccum the Gravel**	
☐	**Check Lighting**	
☐	**Expiration dates** For Kits & Supplies	

ADDITIONAL NOTES

🐟 Tank:		📅 Days/Weeks Since the Last Test:
📅 Date:	🐟 Fish count:	🐟 Fish Lost since the Last Count:
🌵 Fish Behavior:		🐟 Feeding:

Tick Box	Maintenance Check List	Maintenance check details
☐	**Filters Check**	....
☐	**Pumps Check**	....
☐	**Water Level**	....
☐	**Water Temperature**	....
☐	**Tubing Check**	....
☐	**PH Level**	....
☐	**Ammonia**	....
☐	**Nitrite Level**	....
☐	**Nitrate Level**	....
☐	**Phosphate Level**	....
☐	**Carbonate Hardness**	....
☐	**Salinity Level**	....
☐	**Calcium Level**	....
☐	**Water Change** 10-15%	....
☐	**Vaccum the Gravel**	....
☐	**Check Lighting**	....
☐	**Expiration dates** For Kits & Supplies	....

ADDITIONAL NOTES

	Tank:		Days/Weeks Since the Last Test:
	Date:	Fish count:	Fish Lost since the Last Count:
	Fish Behavior:		Feeding:

Tick Box	Maintenance Check List	Maintenance check details
☐	**Filters Check**	
☐	**Pumps Check**	
☐	**Water Level**	
☐	**Water Temperature**	
☐	**Tubing Check**	
☐	**PH Level**	
☐	**Ammonia**	
☐	**Nitrite Level**	
☐	**Nitrate Level**	
☐	**Phosphate Level**	
☐	**Carbonate Hardness**	
☐	**Salinity Level**	
☐	**Calcium Level**	
☐	**Water Change** 10-15%	
☐	**Vaccum the Gravel**	
☐	**Check Lighting**	
☐	**Expiration dates** For Kits & Supplies	

ADDITIONAL NOTES

Tank:		Days/Weeks Since the Last Test:
Date:	Fish count:	Fish Lost since the Last Count:
Fish Behavior:		Feeding:

Tick Box	Maintenance Check List	Maintenance check details
☐	**Filters Check**	
☐	**Pumps Check**	
☐	**Water Level**	
☐	**Water Temperature**	
☐	**Tubing Check**	
☐	**PH Level**	
☐	**Ammonia**	
☐	**Nitrite Level**	
☐	**Nitrate Level**	
☐	**Phosphate Level**	
☐	**Carbonate Hardness**	
☐	**Salinity Level**	
☐	**Calcium Level**	
☐	**Water Change** 10-15%	
☐	**Vaccum the Gravel**	
☐	**Check Lighting**	
☐	**Expiration dates** For Kits & Supplies	

ADDITIONAL NOTES

Tank:		Days/Weeks Since the Last Test:
Date:	Fish count:	Fish Lost since the Last Count:
Fish Behavior:		Feeding:

Tick Box	Maintenance Check List	Maintenance check details
☐	**Filters Check**	
☐	**Pumps Check**	
☐	**Water Level**	
☐	**Water Temperature**	
☐	**Tubing Check**	
☐	**PH Level**	
☐	**Ammonia**	
☐	**Nitrite Level**	
☐	**Nitrate Level**	
☐	**Phosphate Level**	
☐	**Carbonate Hardness**	
☐	**Salinity Level**	
☐	**Calcium Level**	
☐	**Water Change** 10-15%	
☐	**Vaccum the Gravel**	
☐	**Check Lighting**	
☐	**Expiration dates** For Kits & Supplies	

ADDITIONAL NOTES

| Tank: | Days/Weeks Since the Last Test: |

| Date: | Fish count: | Fish Lost since the Last Count: |

| Fish Behavior: | Feeding: |

Tick Box	Maintenance Check List	Maintenance check details
☐	**Filters Check**	....
☐	**Pumps Check**	....
☐	**Water Level**	....
☐	**Water Temperature**	....
☐	**Tubing Check**	....
☐	**PH Level**	....
☐	**Ammonia**	....
☐	**Nitrite Level**	....
☐	**Nitrate Level**	....
☐	**Phosphate Level**	....
☐	**Carbonate Hardness**	....
☐	**Salinity Level**	....
☐	**Calcium Level**	....
☐	**Water Change** 10-15%	....
☐	**Vaccum the Gravel**	....
☐	**Check Lighting**	....
☐	**Expiration dates** For Kits & Supplies	....

ADDITIONAL NOTES

Tank:		Days/Weeks Since the Last Test:

Date:	Fish count:	Fish Lost since the Last Count:

Fish Behavior:		Feeding:

Tick Box	Maintenance Check List	Maintenance check details
☐	**Filters Check**	
☐	**Pumps Check**	
☐	**Water Level**	
☐	**Water Temperature**	
☐	**Tubing Check**	
☐	**PH Level**	
☐	**Ammonia**	
☐	**Nitrite Level**	
☐	**Nitrate Level**	
☐	**Phosphate Level**	
☐	**Carbonate Hardness**	
☐	**Salinity Level**	
☐	**Calcium Level**	
☐	**Water Change** 10-15%	
☐	**Vaccum the Gravel**	
☐	**Check Lighting**	
☐	**Expiration dates** For Kits & Supplies	

ADDITIONAL NOTES

Are you enjoying this awsome book?

If so, please leave us a review. We are very interested in your feedback to create even better products for you to enjoy in the near future.

Shopping for Aquarium Maintenance Logbook supplies can be fun. Discover our complete collection on our website at www.amazing-notebooks.com, our Amazon Page at http://bit.ly/amazing-notebooks or simply scan the QR code below to see all of our awesome and creative products!

Thank you very much!

Amazing Notebooks

www.amazing-notebooks.com

Printed in Great Britain
by Amazon